A Proposal for Printing in English, the Select Orations of Marcus Tullius Cicero, According to the Last Oxford Edition. Translated by Henry Eelbeck

A
PROPOSAL

For Printing in *English*,

THE

Select Orations

O F

Marcus Tullius Cicero,

According to the laſt *Oxford* Edition.

——*Concedat Laurea linguæ.*

Tranſlated by

HENRY EELBECK.

L O N D O N,

Printed in the Year 1715.

Advertisement.

THIS Book will be printed on the same Paper and Letter with the Specimen; and is proposed to be delivered to Subscribers at *Half a Guinea*; *Five Shillings* in Hand, and the Remainder on the Delivery of a perfect Book in Quires.

N. B. If due Encouragement be given to this Work; the Copy being all ready, 'twill be forthwith sent to the Prefs, in order to be delivered to the Subscribers against *Christmas* next.

The first Oration, which is in Behalf of Aulus Licinius Archias the Poet.

The ARGUMENT.

Syllan *and* Carbo *had made a Law, that those should be accounted* Roman Citizens, *who had been inroll'd in the confederate Cities, and had a Dwelling-House in* Italy, *at that Time when the Law was made, and avouched the same within sixty Days before the Prætor.* Mov'd *by this Law, one* Giacchus *accus'd* Archias *the Poet in publick Judgment, that he pretended himself to be a Citizen in the City, when he was not a Citizen. For he deny'd* Archias *to be upon Record in the confederate Cities, and at the Time of the Law made by* Syllan *and* Carbo *to have had a Mansion-House in* Italy, *and to have avouched it before the Prætor.*

Cicero,

Cicero, *as he entirely lov'd the Poet, defends him with this Oration, in a great Resort and Concourse of learned Men.*

And first of all he proves, that Archias *was a legal Citizen, since he was inroll'd at* Heraclea, *as well as other Cities; and at that time when the Law was made, had a Dwelling-House in* Italy; *and, in fine, had avouched the same before the Prætor.*

Then considering the Cause was but trifling of it self, he makes a Digression to the common Topick of the Studies of Literature, and to the Praise of Archias, *by which he perswades the Judges, that* Archias, *altho' he was not a Citizen, yet he ought to be made free of the City, because of his great Learning, and Merits towards the People of* Rome.

And because it seem'd new and absurd in a publick Court, to enter into the Commendations of Learning, and the Person accus'd, Cicero *excuseth himself in his Exordium, because he introduced a new Way of pleading into the* Forum, *contrary to the Custom of Courts of Judicature. This is the judicial kind of Oration, but the State of it is conjectural, whether* Archias *be a free Denizen of* Rome? *This he confirms by Witnesses and Records, and confutes all Objections.*

Impartial

Impartial Judges!

F there be any natural Ingenuity in my Power, which
I perceive very small; or if
there be any frequent Pra-
ctice of Pleading, in which
I own that I have not been
meanly conversant, or if there be any Reason of this Matter depending, to be drawn
from the Studies of the best Arts and Di-
scipline, wherein I own the greatest Part of
my Life to have been employ'd, This
A Licinius Archias here ought almost by
his own Right and Merit to claim the Benefit and Advantage of all these *Qualifi-
cations.*

For as far as my Mind is able to review
the Space of my past Life, and to make the
farthest Remembrance of my Childhood,
considering from that time unto this, I perceive Him to have been the principal Person
that mov'd me both to the Undertaking,
and entering upon the Course of those
Studies

But if this Way of Pleading hath at any
Time been an Advantage to some Persons,
conformable with the Advice, and Instru-
ctions of this Man, of whom we have re-
ceived that Benefit, whereby we were able
to relieve some, and preserve others, truly
we ought both to vindicate and justifie this
very *Gentleman,* as much as lies in our
Power.

And left any one fhould admire, perhaps,
that I fay thus; becaufe this Man's Faculty
30 is of a different Nature, and not of this
Method of Pleading or Difcipline: We
our felves indeed have not all of us been
ever entirely add &ed to this kind of Study.

For all Arts which appertain to Humanity, have fome common Connexion, and as
it were, are link'd together by a fort of
Kindred, or Relation.

35 But left it fhould feem a Surprize to
any of you, that I ufe this kind of Ora-
tory in a legal Debate, and in a publick
Affembly, when the Caufe is controverted
before the Prator, the moft felect Man of
the *Roman* People, and before the ftricteft
Judges, in fo great a Convention and Re-
fort of learned Men; which is not only
5 contrary to the Cuftom of judicial Proceed-
ings, but alfo to the Way of Pleading in
Courts.

I beg of you, that in this Caufe, you
would grant me this Liberty, fuited to the
Caufe of this Defendant, without being
troublefome to you, as I hope, that in this
Concourfe of moft learned Men, out of your
fingular Humanity, and before this Prator,
10 in fine, giving his Judgment, you would fuf-
fer me, I fay, pleading for the greateft Poet,
and the greateft Scholar, to fpeak a little
more freely of the Studies of Humanity,
and ingenious Literature: And in Defence
of fuch a Perfon, who, becaufe of his Eafe
and Employment, has been very little Con-
15 verfant in judicial Matters, and Dangers, to
make

make ufe of almoft a new and unufual kind of Eloquence

But, and if I may think that Liberty allow'd me, and granted by you, truly I fhall make it appear, that this *A Licinius* ought not only not to be feparated from the Number of Citizens, fince he is a Citizen; but alfo that if he was not, you ought in your own Judgment to make him one upon Record.

For fo foon as *Archias* came to Maturity, and left off ftudying thofe Arts, by which our Childhood ufes to be train'd up to Humanity, he betook himfelf to the Bufinefs of writing.

Firft at *Antioch*, (for there he was born in a noble Place, and once a famous, and plentiful City, and abounding with moft learned Men, as well as moft liberal Studies) it happened that he foon excell'd all others in the Glory of his Wit. Afterwards in other Parts of *Afia*, and all over *Greece*, his Arrival was fo much celebrated, that the Expectation of the Man exceeded the Fame of his Wit, and his Coming with their Admiration furpafs'd the Expectation of his Arrival.

Italy at that Time abounded with the Arts and Difciplines of *Greece*, and thofe Studies alfo were more eagerly cultivated in *Latium*, than they are now in the fame Towns, and at *Rome* here, they were not neglected, becaufe of the Tranquillity of the State

And therefore both the *Tarentines*, and *Rhegians*, and the *Neapolitanes*, infranchis'd him, with other Marks of their Bounty and

A 4 Efteem,

Esteem, and even all Men, who were able
to judge any thing of his Wit and Parts,
thought him worthy of their Acquaintance
and Familiarity.

5   Being so much celebrated for his great
Fame, and known even to those that never
saw him, he came to *Rome* in the Consul-
ship of *Marius*, and *Catulus* He first got
the Favour of both those Consuls, one of
which gave Ear to his Writing of the greatest Affairs, as they were transacted, the
10 other also employ'd him to write down
the Records of State, as well as his own
Studies.

Immediately the *Luculli*, at that time when
A ch as also wore the Purple Robe of State,
receiv'd him into their own Family. But
this was not only owing to his great Wit,
and good Learning, but also to his good
Nature, prudent Conduct and Virtue, so
that the House which had been the first
15 Encourager of his Youth, was still the most
friendly to his old Age

In those Days he was delightful to *Q.*
Metellus the *Numidian*, and to his Son *Pius*;
he was entertain'd of *M Æmilius* as his In-
structor, He liv'd with *Q. Catulus*, both Fa-
ther and Son, He was kindly respected by
L Crassus · but he was very greatly honour'd
20 when he oblig'd the *Luculli*, and *Drusus*, and
the *Octavii*, and *Cato*, and the whole Family
of the *Hortensii*, by his Acquaintance and
Conversation So that they who desired
either to hear or understand any thing,
did not only reverence him; but also even
they, who perhaps did only dissemble.

In

In the mean time, when he was gone 25
a great Way with *L. Lucullus* into *Cilicia*,
and when he departed out of that Province
with the same *Lucullus*, he came a long Jour-
ney to *Heraclea*, which being a City go-
vern'd by the most equitable Laws, and
the justest Alliance, he was willing to be
made free of that Corporation; and as he
was thought worthy of it by his own Merit, he easily obtain'd it of the *Heracleans*, 30
by the Favour and Authority of *Lucullus*.

This Freedom was granted by the Law
of *Sylla* and *Carbo*, if any Persons had been
inroll'd in the confederate Cities, if they
had a Mansion-House in *Italy* at that time,
when the Law was made, and they had 35
avouch'd it before the Prætor within sixty
Days · seeing that *Archias* had for many
Years a Mansion-House at *Rome*, and did
avouch it before the Prætor, *Q Metelus*,
his most familiar Friend. If we speak of
nothing else, but his Freedom and the Law;
I have no more to say, the Cause is our own!

For which of these Arguments, *Gracchus* !
can you refute? Will you deny him to be   5
upon Record at *Heraclea* ? *L. Lucullus* is in
Court, a Gentleman of very great Authority, Conscience, and Integrity, who says
he does not only think t, but knows it;
that he did not hear it, but saw it; that
he was not only present, but acted and ma- 10
naged the Affair himself

The Commissioners of *Heraclea* are in
Court too, very noble Men, who came hi-
ther upon the Account of this Trial, with
their Credentials and publick Authority, and
they

they affirm that he was inroll'd, and upon
Record at *Heraclea*.

Here you ask for the Regiſters and Records
15 of the *Heracleans*, which we all know were
loſt in the *Italick* War, when the Exche-
quer was burnt. And 'tis ridiculous to ſay
nothing of thoſe Vouchers which we have,
and to enquire for thoſe things, which we are
not able to produce; and not to ſpeak of
the Remembrance of Men, but importu-
nately to demand the Memorial of Deeds.
And when you have the Teſtimony of a
20 very honourable Gentleman, as well as the
Oath a d Fidelity of a moſt uncorrupted
Incorporation; to rejeɫt theſe things, which
by no Means can be miſinterpreted, or
depraved; and to ask for Writings and In-
ſtruments, which you your ſelf affirm are
frequently corrupted and falſifyed.

Had he not a Manſion-Houſe at *Rome?*
He, who for ſo many Years before the Freedom was granted him, made *Rome* the Founda-
25 tion of all his Concerns, and the Seat of
his own Fortune? But did he not avouch
it? He did certifie it by thoſe Records,
which alone from that Certificate, and
Court of the Prætors, have the Authority
of publick Statutes?

30 For when the Records of *Appius* were ſaid
to be more negligently kept than was fit-
ting, the Levity of *Gabinus*, ſo long as it
was out of Danger, and his Calamity after
Condemnation, had cancell'd all the Credit
of the Statute-Books and Records, *Metellus*,
a moſt devout, and the modeſteſt of all Men,
35 took ſuch great Care, that he came to *L.*
Lentulus

Lentulus the Prætor, and to the Judges, and said that he was extremely concern'd at the blotting of one Name. But in these Registers, you see no Blur or Mark of Disgrace upon the Name of *A. Licinius.* And since Matters are so, what is the Reason that you should doubt of his Freedom? especially, since he hath been inroll'd in other incorporate Towns.

For since Men in *Greece* frankly bestow'd Freedoms *gratis* upon many mean Persons, that were qualify'd, either with none, or very mean Employments, I am of Opinion that the *Rheginians*, or *Locrensians*, or *Neapolitans*, or the *Tarentines*, wou'd not have refused the Privilege to this Poet, endu'd with the most excellent Character of good natural Parts, which they us'd to bestow on those Drudges and Mechanicks that dress'd up their Theaties.

Why? Since some not only after their Freedom granted, but also after the *Papian-Law*, by some means or other, have crept into the publick Writings of their incorporated Towns, shall he be rejected that does not make use even of those Registers, wherein he is inroll'd, because he always had a mind to be reckon'd an *Heraclean*? Without doubt you will ask for the Valuation of our Substance, forsooth! But 'tis a thing unknown to the succeeding Censors, that accompanied that most renown'd General *L. Luculus* with his Army in the Time of the former Censors; that he was with him, when he was Quæstor or Treasurer in *Asia*, *Julius* and *Crassus* being the first; and that no

part

20 part of the People was then cefs'd, valu'd,
or regifter'd.   .   .   .

But becaufe this Valuation does not cor-
roborate the Freedom of the City, and
barely fhews that he who is valued did then
pretend himfelf to be a Citizen, in thofe
Days which you complain of, and that his
Judgment truly was unacquainted with the
Rites and Privileges of the *Roman* Citizens
He hath often both made his Will accor-
25 ding to our Laws, and hath enter'd upon
Inheritances of *Roman* Citizens; and among
his other Privileges, has been brought to
the Publick Treafury by *L. Lucullus*, both
being Prætor and Conful.   .

Seek for other Objections if you can,
30 for he never will be convicted here, neither
in his own Judgment, nor by that of his
Friends. You'll ask of us, *Gracchus*, why
we are fo vehemently delighted with this
Man? Why? becaufe he relieves us with
his Converfation, both when the Mind
ought to be refrefh'd after the Noife of
the Court, and when our Ears tired with
35 wrangling ought to have fome Refpire and
Reft. Do you think that it is poffible to
help us? feeing that we are daily embroil-
ed in fuch a vaft Variety of Actions, unlefs we improve our Minds by Learning,
or can our Minds be able to endure fo
great a Jangling and Contention, unlefs we
refrefh them with the fame Learning? But
I own that I have given my Mind to thefe
Studies; let it afhame others, if there be
any, who have fo buried themfelves in
Letters, that they can neither contribute

any

any thing to their common Profession, nor
bring their Learning into Light and Ap-
pearance.

But why should it ashame me? who
have liv'd thus so many Years, *Judicious Au-
ditors,* that from these Employments no
Profit nor Leisure hath ever obstructed me,
no Pleasure hath given me any Avocation,
nor even sleep it self hath retarded my
Application.

Wherefore, who can finally reproach me,
or who can with just Reason be offended
at me; if as much time as is granted to
others to discharge their own Affairs, as
much as is given to keep up their Plays on
Holy-Days, as much as is allow'd to en-
joy their Pleasures, and for the Rest of
the Body, and the Refreshment of the Mind;
as much as some set apart for intemperate
Banquets, as much as others take, lastly, for
playing at Dice, and at Ball; I shall employ
so much Time to improve these Studies?

And this is so much the more to be granted me, because that from these Studies this
Speech and the Faculty of it proceeds,
which, how mean soever it is in me, hath never been wanting upon the Tryals of my
Friends. Which if any think trifling, I
certainly perceive from what Fountain I
shall draw those Things which really are
Principal.

For unless from my Youth, I had per-
suaded my self, through the Precepts and
great Learning of many Men, that nothing
was so much to be desired in this Life,
as Commendation and Honesty, But that

in Purfuance of thofe Excellencies, all the
30 Tortures of the Body, all the Dangers of
Death and Banifhment, were to be efteem'd
of little Moment· I had never expos'd my
felf for your Safeguard, to fo many, and
fo great Encounters, and to the daily In-
fults of profligate Men. But all Books are
35 full of thofe things, the Words of wife
Men are full of 'em, the Antiquity of Ex-
amples are full of 'em, which had all laid
in Darknefs, unlefs the Light of Learning
had publifh'd them.

How many Writers, both *Greek* and *La-*
tin, have left us the Effigies of the braveft
Heroes drawn out at length, not only for
our Infpection, but alfo our Imitation?
Which I always fetting before me in the
5 Government of the State, did conform my
Mind and Inclination, according to the
Confiderations of thefe excellent Men?

Some Perfon will afk, What! were
not thofe great Men themfelves, whofe
Virtues are deliver'd down in Writing, in-
ftructed in that Learning which you praife
10 and extol? It is hard to prove this of
them all, but yet I am refolv'd what to
anfwer

I own that there have been many Men of
an excellent Courage and Conduct, who,
without Learning, have appear'd of them-
15 felves both temperate and grave, by the
Habit of Nature her felf almoft divine.
I add, that Nature without Learning has
oftener conduc'd more to Praife and Virtue,
than Learning without Nature. And I contend for the fame, that when fome certain

tain Reafon and Corroboration of Learn- 20
ing hath improv'd an excellent and illuftri-
ous Nature, then fomething that is fingular and remarkable happens to appear:
Of this Number was that Divine *Africanus,*
whom our Forefathers faw; of this, *C. Læ-*
lius, L. Furius, very modeft and fober Men; 25
of this, the braveft Man, and the moft
learned in thofe Days, *M. Cato* the Elder;
who truly, had they not been affifted by
Learning to perceive and adore Virtue,
had never betaken themfelves to the Study
of it.

But if in this Cafe fo great an Advan- 30
tage did not appear, and if from thofe Studies, Delight only was defired, yet am I
of Opinion, you would judge this the
moft humane and liberal Diverfion of the
Mind. For the other Studies are not pro-
per for all Times, nor for all Ages, nor
Countries.

Thefe Studies nurfe up Youth, delight 35
old Age, adorn Profperity, yield a Re-
fuge and Comfo t to thofe in Adverfity, Delight at home, do not hinder abroad,
fpend whole Nights, travel abroad, and
dwell in the Country with us But if we
our felves were not able to reach thofe
things, nor tafte them with our own
Senfes; yet fhould we admire them, when 5
we fee them in others.

Which of us was of fuch a favage and
hard hearted a Difpofition, that was not
concern'd lately at the Death of *Rofcius* ?
who, although he died old, yet for his excellent

cellent Art and Grace of speaking, seem'd
10 to deserve not to die at all.

If he then had procur'd himself so great
an Affection of us all by the Deportment
of his Body ; shall we neglect the incre-
15 dible Motions of our Minds, and the Quick-
ness of our Wits? How often have I seen
this *Archias*, may it please you, my Judges,
(for I will trespass on your Patience, because you attend me so diligently in this
new Way of Pleading) How often have I
20 seen him, without writing a Letter, speak
a great Number of very excellent Verses
Extempore, concerning those very Occur-
rences which were then in Agitation!
How often recollect himself, and speak the
same thing in different Words and Sentences!
But those which he had writ accurately and
with Deliberation, I have seen so strictly
25 examined and approved, that they came up
to the Praise of the ancient Writers.

May I not love this Man? May I not
admire him ? May I think not to maintain
his Cause with all the Arguments in my
Power? But so have we receiv'd it from the
greatest and the most learned Men, that
the Studies of our other Employments are
discovered by Learning, Instruction, and Art ·
But a Poet excels by Nature it self, and
is excited by the Energy of his own Mind,
and as it were divinely insp red.

30 Wherefore our *Ennius* calls the Poets
Holy, by his own Authority, that they may
seem recommended to us, as it were, by some
Gift and Inspiration of the Gods. And
35 therefore, my Lords, let this Name of *Poet*
be

be facred amongft you, the moft ingenious of Men, which no Barbarity hath ever yet violated. Rocks and Deferts anfwer with an Eccho; Savage Beafts are oftentimes chaim'd and ftand amaz'd at their Harmony: Can we that are train'd up to the beft of Things, not be mov'd with the heavenly Voice of Poets?

The *Colophonians* claim *Homer* as their own free Denizen, the *Chians* challenge him as theirs, the *Salaminians* demand him again for their own, but the *Smyrneans* affert him to be their natural born Citizen; and therefore have alfo dedicated a Temple to him in their Town of *Smyrna.* There are a great many befides at Daggers-drawing among themfelves, and contend for him.

If they then demand a Stranger who was a Poet to be theirs, even after his Death, fhall not we accept of this *living One,* who both by his own good Will, and to the Laws, is *ours* already? Efpecially, fince *Archias* formerly bent all his Study, and all his Genius, to celebrate the Glory and Praife of the *Roman* People.

For even when he was a Youth, he touch'd upon the Affairs of the *Cymbri,* and was delightful to *C. Marius* himfelf, who feem'd lefs inclin'd to thofe Studies. For there is not any one fo averfe to the *Mufes,* who cannot eafily bear with an Everlafting Encomium of their own Atchievements committed to Verfe

They report that *Themiftocles,* a very great Man at *Athens,* when he was ask'd, what Lecture, or whofe Difcourfe, he could moft

B

willingly

willingly hear? anfwer'd, of *Him*, by whom
h's own Virtues fhould be moft excellently
fet forth.

And therefore, *Marius* alfo exceedingly
lov'd *L. Pottus*, by whofe Wit he thought
thofe Exploits which he had done could
be celebrated and kept in everlafting Remembrance. But his great and difficult War
w'th *Mithridates*, carry'd on by Sea and
Land, with great Variety of Fortune, is
all writ by *him*; which Writings do not only
make *L. Lucullus* a moft valiant and renowned General, but alfo illuftrate the very Name
of the *Roman* People

For the *Roman* People, under the Command of *Lucullus*, open'd the Way to *Pontus*,
formerly fortify'd both with Royal Wealth,
and by the natural Situation of the Country, The Army of the *Romans*, under the
Command of the fame General, with a very fmall *Handful of Men*, routed the innu-
merable Troops of the *Armenians* 'Tis the
Honour of the *Roman* People, that the moft
amicable City of the *Cizicent*, was by h's
Conduct, as well freed from any Attack of
the King, as refcu'd and preferv'd from the
Mouth and Jaws of the whole War. Our
City will always be prais'd and extoll'd
for it *L. Lucullus* fighting with the Ene-
my in a Naval-Battle, having flain their
Commanders, their vanquifh'd Fleet, and
that incredible Sea-fight at *Tenedos*, are
our *Trophes*, our Monuments, our Triumphs
Wherefore by whofe Ingenuity thofe Affairs
are publickly releas'd, by them the Fame
of the People of *Rome* is celebrated

Our

Our *Ennius* was dearly belov'd by *Africa- nus* the Elder. And therefore in the Sepulchre of the *Scipio's* he is suppos'd to be set up in Marble. But certainly, by those Praises not only they who are commended, but also the Name of the *Roman* People is highly adorn'd. *Cato* his Great-Grandfather is canoniz'd: Great Honour is done to the Affairs of the *Roman* People; and in fine, all those famous Men, the *Maximi*, the *Marcelli*, the *Fulvii*, are graced and decorated not without the common Praise of us all.

What then did our Ancestors receive that famous Man *Rudius* into the Freedom, who had done those things? And shall we reject this *Heraclean* out of our City, earnestly desir'd by many Corporations, but qualify'd by the Laws at *Heraclea*?

For if any one imagins that a lesser Glory is to be reapt from *Greek* Verse, than the *Latin*, he is in a gross Mistake; because that the *Greek* is read almost in all Countries; the *Latin* is confin'd within its own Limits, and those very narrow ones. Wherefore if those Exploits which we have done be limited to some Countries of the Universe; we ought to covet to carry our Glory and Fame, whither our Arms have not yet penetrated; because as those things are *Honourable* to those People themselves, whose Transactions are written; they are certainly the greatest Encouragement both of Perils and Labours to those, who venture their Lives in fighting for Glory.

How

How many Writers of his own Tranf-
actions is *Alexander* the *Great* reported to
have had along with him? and yet when
he was standing in *Sigeum* at *Achilles's*
35 Tomb, says he, O fortunate Young-Man!
who hast found *Homer* the *Encomiaft* of thy
Virtue! And for very good Reason; for
unlefs his *Iliad* had been publifh'd, the
fame Tomb which cover'd his Body, had
also over-whelm'd his Name. What did
our own great Hero, who equall'd Fortune
with his Valour?

Did not he at a publick Court-Marfhal,
5 make free or infranchize *Theophanes* of *Myti-
lene*, the Writer of his Affairs; and thofe
val ant brave Men of ours, but Rufticks
and Soldiers, excited by the fweet Charms
of Glory, as if they had been Partakers
10 of his Praife, approv'd of his Freedom with
lowd Acclamations?

And therefore, I am of Opinion, if *Archias* was not a *Roman* Citizen according to
the Laws; he could not prevail with
any General to make him free of the City.
I believe, when *Scylla* infranchiz'd the *Spa-
niards* and *French*, that he rejected him ask-
ing for his Freedom.

When a bad Poet had fubmitted a Book
to him concerning the People, which we
15 faw in this Affembly, becaufe he had only
made an Epigram upon him in Hexameter
and Pentameter-Verfe, he immediately order'd
the Man, for the Trafh he then fold, a
Reward to be given him, upon that Condi-
tion he fhould not write any thing afterwards. Would not he who thought the
Poetafter's

Poetaster's Diligence worthy of some Re-20
ward, have desir'd to see this Poet's Wit, both
his Power and his Copiousness in Writing?
What! could not he have obtain'd his
Freedom of *Metellus Pius,* his most familiar
Friend, who infranchiz'd many People; nei-25
ther by his own Interest, nor the Interces-
sion of the *Luculli?* Which things especially he so much desired to be written concerning his own Affairs, that he lent an
Ear even to the Poets born at *Corduba*
writing their *Bombast,* some foreign Stuff,
and nothing to the Purpose.

Neither is this to be dissembled, which
cannot be hid, but must be discover'd, 30
that we are all led on by the Desire of
Praise; and the best of us all is very much
captivated with Glory. The Philosophers
themselves inscribe their own Names even
to those Treatises, which they write concerning the Contempt of Glory And in
that very thing whereby they despise Osten-35
tation and Nobility, would have themselves
praised, and their Names renowned.

Indeed *Decimus Burcus,* that excellent Man,
and famous General, hung the Entrances of
his own Temples and Monuments with
the Poems of his dearly beloved Friend *At-
tius.* And ever since, *Fulvius,* who made War 5
with the *Etolians,* having *Ennius* for his
Companion, doubted to dedicate his martial
Spoils to the Muses.

Wherefore in what City soever the Generals almost in Armour have reverenc'd
the Name of the Poets, and the Temples
of the Muses, in that Place the Judges
adorn'd

adorn'd with their Gowns ought not to
10 dishonour the Muses, and eschew the Pa-
tronage of Poets. And that you, my Judges, may do that more willingly, I will now
declare my self to you, and acknowledge
a certain Love I have of Glory, too forward
a one perhaps, but yet honest. For what-
ever Affairs we have transacted in our Con-
sulship together with you, for the Safety
15 of th s City and Empire, both for the Lives
o cur Countrymen, and for the whole Go-
ver ment; *Archias* has touch'd upon in
Verse, and begun the Work. Upon hearing
of which, that was agreeable to me, and
seem'd a great Performance, I encourag'd
20 h m to fi ish it. For Virtue asks no other
Re vard of Labours and Toils, besides this
of Praise and Glory, which indeed being
taken away, my Lords! What Reason is
there that in so small a Stage of Life, and
so short, we should employ our selves in
25 so great Hardships? Without Doubt, if
the Mind did foresee nothing for the Fu-
ture, and if the Space of this Life was cir-
cumscrib'd within some Regions, it would ter-
minate all its Thoughts there; and would
not fat gue it self with so great Labours,
nor be troubled with so many Cares and
30 Watchings, neither would it contend so
often for Life t self.

Now there is fix'd in every good Man, a
certain Virtue, which stirs up his Mind
Night and Day with a Desire of Glory,
and admonishes him that the Commemora-
tion of our Names ought not to be dif-
miss'd with the Term of Life, but con-
tinued to all Posterity   But

But can we all be of fo little Courage, who 35
are employ'd in the State, and in thele Perils and Hardfhips of Life, that when we have
not led our Lives quiet and eafy, until the very laft Moment of 'em, we fhould think that
all things would die together with us? Since
that many very great Men have induftrioufly 5
behind 'em left Statues and Images, not the
Refemblances of theirMinds, but of their Bo-
dies, ought not we much more defire to leave
the Effigies of our Councils and Virtues pour-
tray'd and polifh'd by the greateft Wits? But
I did fuppofe that I fcatter'd and difpers'd
all the things which I tranfacted even then in
the very Attempt of 'em, to the everlafting
Remembrance of the whole Univerfe 10

But whether thefe things fhall be wanting
to my Senfe after Death; or, as the moft wife
Men have thought, will belong to fome part
of my own Mind, at prefent truly I am de- 15
lighted with fome Foretafte andHope ofthem.

Wherefore, moft impartial Judges! Save
the Man of thatModefty, both for his Worth,
and for his own decent Behaviour, whom you
fee approv'd of by the Studies of his Friends;
but of fo great a Wit, as that is convenient
to be efteem'd, which you may fee defired by
the natural Difpofitions of the greateft Men,
and whofe Caufe may be evidently prov'd by
the Benefit of the Law, the Authority of the 20
Corporation, the Teftimony of *Lucullus,* and
the Records of *Metel'us*

And fince Matters ftand fo, we beg of you,
my Lords, if there ought to be any Commendation, not only humane, but alfo divine, in
fuch great Concerns, that you would take

Archias

Archias into your own Protection, that he may seem to be rather favour'd thro' your singular Humanity, than misused by too rigid a Severity, Him, who hath celebrated you, who hath celebrated your Generals, who hath always adorn'd the Transactions of the *Roman* People; who also in these fresh domestick Dangers of ours and yours, professes that he will give an everlasting Testimony of your Praises; and who is one of that Number, which have always been accounted and pronounced *Sacred* by all Men: For which Reason, according to my Custom, I've spoken briefly and in plain Terms: My Lords, I hope these Arguments are approv'd by you all, what I have advanc'd, not according to the Custom of the *Forum*, nor in a Judicial Manner, both of the Gentleman's Wit and Study in common, *that* I hope, my Lords! you will take in good part: In my own Judgment, I am fully satisfy'd he that passes Sentence, will.

F I N I S.